"This book is the prescription church leaders need in large doses. Eric Konohia and Andrew P. Surace deliver this 'new norm' for safeguarding houses of worship."

Paul Michael Viollis Sr, CEO
Viollis Group International

SECURING THE SACRED

Making Your House of Worship A Safer Place

Dr. Andrew P. Surace
Eric Konohia, CMAS, CMEPS

© Copyright 2016 Andrew Surace and Eric Konohia

All rights reserved. No part of this book may be reproduced, stored in a retrieval system, or transmitted in any form or by any means – electronic, mechanical, photocopying, recording, or otherwise – without the prior written permission of the publisher and the copyright owner. The only exception is brief quotations in printed reviews.

7710-T Cherry Park Dr, Ste 224

Houston, TX 77095

www.WorldwidePublishingGroup.com

The views expressed in this book are those of the author and do not necessarily reflect those of the publisher.

eBook: 978-3-9602-8051-4

Paperback: 978-0692727430

Hardcover: 978-1-60796-539-8

Dedication

This book is dedicated to all the men and women who have lost their lives on Holy Grounds. While it seems like most have gone un-noticed by the World they have not been un- noticed by Heaven, Tertullian said it beautifully when he said, "The blood of the martyrs is the seed of the church."

Most recently our dear brothers and sisters who lost their lives in Charleston while ministering to a very disturbed young man, your blood is already bringing about great change in our nation. The Bible says precious in the sight of the Lord is the death of His saints. While the enemy thinks he is destroying the church he is actually helping build it. This can only happen in a super-natural Kingdom.

May all who read this book remember that while there are many things we can do to protect ourselves, in the end our greatest protection is God and it is to Him we give all the glory for this book.

Co-author Dedication
Eric Konohia

I dedicate this book to God for my gifts and my calling in life.

    To my mother, Mary E. Konohia, who was always in my corner, and my father, Philip P. Konohia, who gave me my drive, work ethic and taught me the principles of life. Me ke kipona Aloha Nui loa!!!!

    To my wife, Diana – My Angel, who never gave up on me and has always supported my aspirations.

    To my children, Kaleo, Hiapo and Ioela, you are my strength and have allowed me to share life's lessons given to me and continue my rich Hawaiian heritage.

    To my siblings, Carolyn, Joe, Deborah, Jerry and Kuulei, you have always believed in me in every station in my life. I pray that I continue to make you proud.

    To my sister-in-law, Aisha Kane Washington, JD for coming through at the last minute to review and edit the legal considerations. Thank you for your legal expertise and experience with providing the same with your own church, Metropolitan UMC, Baltimore, MD

    To Paul Viollis, PhD for being my industry mentor and brother. Thank you for lifting me as you climbed.

Last, but not least, to my granddaughter and Princess Kuliaikanuumana, born on my birthday. [1/9/61 & 1/9/16] The meaning of the name that I gave her is: *To strive to for the summit of spiritual power*, which embraces everything in which I believe.

Co-author Dedication
Dr. Andrew P. Surace

Wired into most pastors is the idea of protection. Usually that idea of protection has much to do with protecting the sheep from bad theology. Bad theology is a relative thing however because it all depends on what you think is good theology.

As a young boy growing up in New York, instilled in me was the idea that people need to be protected. Whether they are on a subway platform or a church platform, the idea of protection has been with me since a child.

After meeting Eric, getting trained as an executive protection specialist along with life guard training as a young man and EMT training I was able to put feet to the many different ways to help protect people in a church setting.

Writing this book has been a labor of love that we both believe will bring forth much fruit. As our culture becomes more and more jaded against both God and the church we have outlined simple, but yet very effective ways to better protect your church or House of Worship.

Over the time it took us to write this book I experienced many personal setbacks and struggles. This book has been a compass to help keep my mind settled on some of the very few things in life that are important. Because people are important protecting them is very important.

I thank the Lord for allowing us to take this journey and protecting us in our efforts to protect. Also thank my wife, Kathleen, whose constant encouragement has kept me going almost 25 years now along with my six precious children who were my first principals.

In the end Psalm 127:1 gives us the bottom line for all our protective instincts... "Unless the Lord builds the house, they labor in vain who build it: Unless the Lord guards the city, the watchman stays awake in vain." May this book be as much a blessing to churches and ministries around the world as it was a great adventure for us to write it!

Table of Contents

CHAPTER ONE
THE GREAT ILLUSION: CHURCH IS A SAFE PLACE............. 15

CHAPTER TWO
CAN FAITH AND SECURITY BE MARRIED?........................... 29

CHAPTER THREE
WHO'S THAT KNOCKING AT MY DOOR - WOLF OR
SHEEP DOG? 41

CHAPTER FOUR
NEW TIMES REQUIRE A NEW MINDSET................................ 51

CHAPTER FIVE
AN EYE FOR AN EYE - THE FORCE CONTINUUM 63

CHAPTER SIX
TROUBLE IN THE OUTER LIMITS.. 73

CHAPTER SEVEN
STUCK IN THE MIDDLE WITH YOU- THE HOLY PLACE..... 83

CHAPTER EIGHT
THE GREAT DISTRACTION 95

CHAPTER NINE
RECOMMENDATIONS AND LEGAL CONSIDERATIONS. 103

GLOSSARY.. 111

FREQUENTLY ASKED QUESTIONS…………………………...115

CONTACT THE AUTHORS…………………………………………121

Introduction

Can church protection and faith be married? Is your church still a safe place? Security Expert Eric Konohia, and Pastor/Protection Specialist for the Church, Andrew P. Surace, answer these and many other questions about why the church in America must begin to look at these difficult issues. Discover...

...what the Bible says about self-protection.

...what are some of the most dangerous times and places in your church.

...why a new mindset is necessary to deal with the uptick in church violence.

...what Jesus meant when He said, "Be wise as serpents and harmless as doves."

...why building a security team does more than just help protect your church.

...simple and effective ways to make your church a harder target from those who mean harm.

...why it does not take a lot of money, but recognizing and training the sheep dogs already in your church.

Historically churches have been safe places where people have come to find peace and comfort. Over the last 15 years statistics on church crime and violence have steadily gone up to the point where today we hear about pastors and church members dealing with violence on an almost regular basis.

This book will walk you through a journey of the why, what and how to make your church a safer place for all who walk through the doors.

Written through the eyes of a pastor and a security expert it is not a book intended to induce fear but to produce preparation and due diligence to make your church safer.

Chapter One
THE GREAT ILLUSION: CHURCH IS A SAFE PLACE

Being the Church has always been a dangerous thing... going to church has not. In the last fifteen years there have been close to eight hundred deadly force incidents (DFI) in American churches with just under five hundred ending in death. Compare that with the fact that in the last thirty years there have been 297 shooting deaths in American schools and you have to wonder why the conversation on church violence has been so little.

Looking back at the how first century Christians lived out their walk with God, it is clear to see that when you took a stand for Christ you took a hit from both the religious world and the local government and culture of that time.

Even more interesting, Jesus knew very well what the dangers of following Him would be and didn't mind having His followers take risks. After all, taking this new message of Good News to the uttermost parts of the earth would involve many risks, both physically, spiritually and even emotionally.

Leaving your family behind to follow Christ was a huge decision which often times you were not given much time to make. After all it was Jesus who said "let the dead bury the dead… you come and follow me" (Luke 9:60).

Considering there were no local police departments, very poor road systems, wild animals, oppressive and corrupt governments, you didn't have to look far for trouble. That doesn't even take into consideration the criminal element of that day, which was certainly abundant.

While being a Christian still brings certain risks and dangers, in many other parts of the world, sitting in a building to worship God with your family shouldn't be one of them.

It is one thing to go and risk your life preaching the Gospel to those who are hungry and lost, but quite another when those who are hungry and lost are put at risk just for listening to you.

I repeat. Jesus did understand that following Him was risky business and this is why He said, "Behold, I send you out as sheep among wolves"(Matt.10: 16).

Sheep are very docile animals with very few defenses. They pretty much depend on a shepherd to keep them safe from any harm or danger. Those dangers could be anything from wild animals looking for a meal, other shepherds trying to steal them to build their own flock, or even their own lack of ability to protect and feed themselves.

The wolves on the other hand, are ruthless and very capable carnivores. They travel in packs and look for the weak and defenseless animal that could be their next meal. Basically what Jesus was saying when He said "I send you out as sheep among wolves" was, "I'm sending you out as dinner."

The early church met in homes where you allow in those you knew and those who knew you. It was not necessarily a public meeting place where all were welcome.

Although Jesus did sometimes teach in the temple, most early Christians met in each other's homes. They even had secret signs and symbols to protect themselves from physical harm such as the "Icthus," what was a symbol that looked very much like a fish. It helped determine where the safe meeting places were, as well as to determine friend from foe. It was in essence the secret handshake; if you didn't know the handshake you did not proceed.

This was the setting of most New Testament worship meetings, the homes of friends and loved ones who would open their home for a time of intimate fellowship and worship of God.

Yes, there was much violence against Christians, but it was more for being a Christian and having dared go against the tide of the local religious strongholds and corrupt governments; not for being in a certain type of building on a certain day of the week. The truth is that today, many people who go to church are not Christians.

The old adage of just because you walk into a garage doesn't make you a car holds very true here in this situation.

This book is not a book on how to hurt or take out the bad guy, but how to change the mindsets of Christians, and pastors, and Christian Leaders to see the potential risks and dangers that lie in the body of Christ and what we can do to mitigate and or be better prepared for times of trouble.

Jesus said that we were blessed when we were persecuted for His name's sake. There is however a huge difference between persecution for His Name's sake and being victims of crime. Jesus had no problem with persecution, He did however not endorse crime.

In Psalm 11:5 it tells us that God hates violence. This book is about how to recognize the possibility of violence and how to ward it off before it comes to fruition.

The Ten commandments are basically laws (which Jesus came to fulfill and build on not to change) that God set up to show His feelings about certain behaviors that were both sins and that today we know as crimes.

Along with the laws God stated, He also determined the punishment of those very sins/crimes. Interestingly, much of our legal system today is based on the Ten Commandments as well as other Old Testament laws, which is why the scrolls of the Ten Commandments until recently have been displayed in many courthouses as well as buildings in Washington and all over the country.

Do not steal (rob), do not murder, do not bear false witness (perjury) teach us that God did not expect anyone, and that would certainly include His own children, to be victims or perpetrators of these crimes.

To be attacked while preaching the Gospel in many ways is not unusual and could even be expected, especially in certain parts of the world. To try to eliminate those attacks when possible, especially attacks on those sheep who have come to be fed, should also be expected and should be a part of our responsibilities as shepherds and church leaders. A shepherd was not just responsible for feeding the sheep, but protecting them from the wolves and other wild animals that saw them as easy prey.

Again, this is not a book about retribution. This book is about having a change of mindset to look for avoidance as well as mitigation of the risks and dangers. These can occur to believers in the body of Christ, especially when they are in their houses of worship.

Self-defense and survival is one of the most natural things wired into humans as well as just about every animal. Some animals do not have great fighting tools, but they have great survival instincts. Rabbits have holes, birds have trees, and turtles have shells.

Self-protection is somehow wired into every living organism. Some can protect themselves by attacking, others have great sensitivity and abilities to discern danger and know how to avoid it.

Some can run fast. Some have a keen sense of smells. Others can climb high but no matter what, they all take the best precautions their instincts and physical prowess allow them to protect themselves. From these examples, we see even nature itself allows for some source of self-protection; Why shouldn't God's people follow suit?

Jesus put it this way in Matthew 10:16, when He told us we should" be wise as serpents and harmless as doves". In essence, what He was saying was being wise enough to keep from getting hurt, but in doing so, try not to hurt anyone.

When Satan came to deceive Adam and Eve he came in the form of a serpent. It's hard to say whether the serpent was always a deceptive animal by nature or became so when controlled by Satan. In either case He was very cunning in speaking with Eve, and this is the basis of this statement by Christ.

Whether it is preparing for a trip out of town or a home remodel, the more prepared we are, the more problems we can avoid and the less chance we have of needing to take extreme measures.

Very much like the secret service model, the idea of church security should be to take every advantage and use every gifting within the body to prevent problems before they become problems. Again to use an old adage, when it comes to church security, an ounce of prevention is worth a pound of cure. It is easier to stand your ground than try to get it back; It is easier to stay healthy than to get well and It is easier to stay off drugs than to get off drugs. The sad truth is that there are some doors in life that once they are opened are incredibly hard to close.

Our thoughts on securing your church are simply this: if I make it hard for you to get in, most likely you will go somewhere else. Most criminals are not looking for a challenge they are looking for a soft touch.

With God' help and by his grace and wisdom the goal of this book is to leave your church in a more secure position so that both the sheep and the shepherd can concentrate on keeping the main thing the main thing.

While there is no such thing as total safety anywhere on this earth, we can as the body of Christ become more safety conscious no matter how small or large our church or church budget.

The sacredness and safety of Heaven are contradicted by the fact that the Church may not be as safe as it used to be. Statistics tell a very concerning story that should not be ignored.

The days where the church house as well as the body of the church were honored, have evolved into days of scorn and opportunity for many with evil on their mind.

During the days of the civil rights movement, the church, because of its lack of security measures, was seen as a place to deliver a message by those who stood against the civil rights movement.

Today, crimes against churches are steadily on the rise. In 2009 Christian Security Network (CSN), *Crimes against Christian Organizations in the United States Report* stated that there were at least 1,237 crimes against Christian churches and ministries in the United States that year. According to the report, there were 12 homicides and 38 other violent incidents that year. These included 3 sexual assaults, 3 kidnappings, 98 arsons and over 700 burglaries.

There is a clear escalation in crimes against the church from the early days compared to today. This by the way does not include a larger number of activities not reported because churches dealt with these incidences internally.

The Federal Bureau of Investigation also tracks crimes against churches and other worship centers as it is a federal matter to carry out a crime against a church. However, experts agree that the FBI's reporting does not accurately account for all crimes against churches.

The FBI lists all reported crimes without the same verification that the CSN does. From that perspective alone, there is a disheartening view on what is reported, and what is reality. During that same year the Bureau reported that 1,376 hate crimes against the Houses of Worship were motivated by religious bias.

Note: This finding was two years before September 11, 2001 and the follow up rhetoric of The War on Terror. In 2010 the CSN reported that there were 1,783 incidents compared to 1,237 in 2009, that's an increase of 546 incidents in one year.

Some may say that's not much, but that's a 69% increase. Each one of those increases represents security and safety flaws that could have been successfully addressed.

The other way you can look at that, is that houses of worship are seen as easy marks, also referred to as soft targets.

If we agree that about 70% of all Christian based churches have less than 100 members, we can surmise that the majority of these incidents occurred at smaller churches

This would also make sense as criminals know that it is the smaller churches that usually have the least amount of people as well as assets set aside for church safety. Whereas the majority of the mega churches have more resources to put into their security and protective measures. This is partly due to their financial capabilities, but it also has to do with a shift in their protective mindset.

The mega churches are also seen as mega targets due to seemingly prosperous lifestyles of many of the well-known pastors as well as the huge and beautiful campuses they are built on. I dare say, even some of the controversial messages delivered at these meetings makes these churches more noticeable and also more of a target.

Did safety in the church ever exist, or did the belief that church may not be a safe place shift once experts took a closer look at the numbers? With information so much more readily accessible, it's probably a little of both. While crimes in general have increased in every area of life as well as the number of people being drawn into a criminal lifestyle. Over the years, sadly, the Church has been no exception.

While violent crimes have become more prevalent overall, it appears that the church may not have changed its mindset as to the thought of how do we become more vigilant and open to protective strategies.

The message of the Bible remains the same in its 66 books within, and is powerfully delivered and proclaimed each time the Church body comes together. However, the message of safety and security has yet to be properly broached perhaps because of the perception that to talk about church safety is a lack of faith.

The wolves in society have not changed over the years, however their tactics have. Stage coach robbers and night riders have been replaced with car thieves, burglars and sexual predators.

Opportunity will always close the gap between reason and motive. How does this relate to the church and the rise in criminal activity over the years? One of the main things that has affected the rise of crime against the church is because the church has gone mainstream.

Fifty years ago you would rarely see a church or a Preacher spreading the gospel on television unless it was a televised funeral or the Reverend Billy Graham consulting a sitting president.

Today there are televised church services every day of the week as well as dedicated television and radio stations for the gospel. Additionally, the total amount of churches has increased exponentially over the years.

Because the church is no longer willing to take a back seat in our culture and has been boldly stepping out to let its voice be heard, it has attracted both the attention of those who have come to Christ as well as His enemies.

In today's culture, the church has risen to rock star status, so to a wolf, it can easily be viewed as another high net-worth opportunity to cash in. The church's modern day elevated status, has brought with it modern day things of value and attraction.

Churches have replaced old paper ledgers with computers, the upright piano and organ with very expensive instruments of all types as well as full blown sound and video systems, all of which can easily be taken to a pawn shop or a local fence for quick monetary exchange usually with no questions asked.

Whether looking at the picturesque days of the small country churches dotted across the fields of gold, the hand chiseled granite corner church, or the campus like mega auditoriums, one thing always remains the same – they all contain people and valuables within and both must be safeguarded.

Inside every church you will find both a land and culture of opportunity which serve as the food that wolves desire and crave. It is there that an emphasis of safety needs to be focused.

In the smaller houses of worship members of the congregation know each other. When a visitor arrives for service, most, if not all, of its members recognize the visitor.

This is a basic form of security: noticing something different or out of place. Today's smaller churches are a mirror of the early church where our grandparents and great grandparents knew everyone in service and recognized who missed the meetings.

Members would make it their business to surround a new visitor and ask [interview/interrogate] them all about themselves. In fact, if Sister Jenkins missed the meeting, it would not be unusual for someone in the church family to check on her welfare. Has the mainstream effect changed the mindset of, "church business" into the business of the Church? In the past, knowing church members and even their personal business, was church business.

The rock star effect has changed how we view the multitudes as the business of the church. While this is relatively new to the church culture, this should not be a frightening issue as solutions are available.

For instance, there has always been some level of understanding, that at some given point of a church meeting, there is money exchanged in the form of an offering.

How that offering is handled from the time of receiving it until it is safely deposited into a bank, has always been a time of vulnerability for the church.

Add to that the number of churches in highly populated areas with little or no church security in place and you can easily see that there is an increase of opportunity and chance, of danger if security and safety procedures are not taken into consideration.

Each member of every congregation, big or small, represents a reason for individual and collective safety concerns.

Value and opportunity are not always in the form of financial gain. In the past, the message from the pulpit carried influence on how people lived their lives. Sunday's message topic helped guide our families as a road-map through life until the next Sunday. It was that beacon of light that our families depended on as a guide to righteous living.

Today the message from the pulpit can have a political and or global focus as well as influence. Just as scripture delivered can have several meanings, the message from the pulpit can be politicized and may change the way others view the church.

This is a relatively new phenomenon that threatens the very core of the church. The truth must be spoken, but may not be received!

The church has been a megaphone for what the Bible teaches is right, but there have been others both inside and outside the church that have perverted that message to use it for their own gain.

Due to the twisting of words and beliefs by a certain few, the mention of the church can raise a flag for safety concerns because of those angry or in disagreement with God's word. That being said we must not water down our message or run from those enemies of the cross.

Instead, we must be prepared for what may lie ahead. You will see as we progress in the book this will provide ministry opportunity as well as a sense of belonging to those who are called to the ministry of protection and safety.

I am in no way alleging that the church is sitting ducks for all criminal activity but we have to ask ourselves two legitimate questions:

How safe are we, and how can we become safer? This book is a guide to help change the church mindset in the area of church safety. To open its eyes not so much to the problem but the solutions.

Chapter Two
CAN FAITH AND SECURITY BE MARRIED?

I find it very interesting that the Bible says very little about church protection, yet the concept of protection runs from Genesis to Revelation. Before you go too far with that thought I might also remind you that the words "trinity" or "rapture" are not in the Bible yet it is filled with allusions to both.

Actually, our churches are filled with many things not listed in the Bible that are not unbiblical. Take for instance air-conditioning, pews, platforms and pulpits. All kidding aside, you don't have to look far to see that one of the primary roles of God is that He is our protector.

Remember, we said in the first chapter that sheep were relatively defenseless animals and when looking for the right animal to describe humanity, Jesus chose sheep. Yes, the idea of protection runs rampant throughout the Bible.

God put fiery angels in front of the tree of life to protect sinful man from eating of it and living forever. Imagine a world where you could get sicker and sicker and never die. God used an ark to protect Noah and his family from the flood. He supernaturally protected the Israelites as they wandered aimlessly through the desert for forty years. He did this in many ways, including supernatural intelligence gathering as well as angelic intervention to help them win wars against their enemies. While God helped Israel supernaturally, they still had to fight. In all things we are called to co-labor with Him.

Like it or not, part of being created in God's image is the desire to protect those we love and to protect ourselves from the enemies we are supposed to love. Yes the wise as serpents' thing is at work again.

As we look at the ideas of protection and safety for the church, the white elephant in the room is "will that conflict with our faith"? Is using certain safety or protective measures to protect God's children as well as our own in conflict with God's will? We will look into this thought using the Bible first to give us guidance and then we will look into our everyday life.

If something is to be good or bad it must be consistently one way or the other. As the book of James tells us, a fountain cannot bring forth both fresh and salt water (James 3:11). If we, the Church of Christ, lock our doors at night, wear seat belts, take medicines, wear bike helmets and take various other protective measures to protect ourselves and those we love, why does it all of a sudden become an issue or worse, a lack of faith if we try to do the same thing inside the church building. This is especially interesting because the reality is we are the church, we just meet at the church house. With that same logic in mind if as Christians we secure our own homes why not a place where we come together to worship God?

Let's be honest, enemies are part of life. The minute you take a stand for anything you will find out who your enemies are. Jesus tells us to love our enemies yet at times He sent the disciples out with swords.

When the high priests and soldiers came to get Jesus, Peter as usual, was the first to act. With one swipe of the sword he cuts off the ear of one of the soldiers. Much to his surprise and embarrassment, Jesus picks up the ear and puts it back on good as new. He then sternly corrects Peter and tells him to put the sword away (not throw it away). He then allows Himself to be taken away by the army of soldiers (John 18:10-11).

There are two things important to note here in this passage: first we see that there are times when for the will of God we must suffer persecution. As we said in the last chapter, preaching the Gospel will often bring persecution. Jesus knew this had to happen to fulfill His destiny which was to die on the cross for the sins of the world. That being said, the other thing to note is that He did not correct Peter for carrying a sword merely for using it at the wrong time. Like everything in life, timing is everything.

I would also mention it was Jesus who told His disciples, if you don't have a sword, sell your cloak and buy one (Luke 22:36). Why would Jesus tell His disciples to buy a sword unless He both understood and agreed with the idea of protecting both themselves and others if the situation arose?

The most often used name for God in the Old Testament, is The Lord of Hosts; that word hosts, in the Hebrew is armies. He is the Lord of the armies.

The heart of God has always been to protect His children in every way both mentally, physically and spiritually. While God is primarily our main protector and no protection can be successful without Him, like many areas of our faith, there are certain things He expects us to do to help take part in our own destinies. Faith without works is dead.

While there are many examples in the Old Testament of God helping the Israelites fight battles against their enemies (one of my favorites was David and Goliath) let me bring one last but very interesting one to light.

When Nehemiah was rebuilding the walls of Jerusalem (Nehemiah 4:13-18) each man carried weapons; swords, spears and bows and were commanded to fight for their wives, children and each other. Another verse in that chapter says that with one hand a man would work and the other he would hold his weapon. Clearly this was not aggression, but protection. While one Day our Lord tells us the lion will lay down with the lamb, it is clear we are not there yet.

"The doors of the church are wide open." This is the last statement I remember at the end of every service I attended. It was that time in the service where the pastor invited the non-believer to accept Christ as his or her personal Savior. It was also that time that the pastor also invited those who were already saved to join the church as a new member.

The irony of this statement is that the doors of the Church *really* are open, in the sense that they are not locked. Historically Churches do not lock their doors so that anyone can come in and hear the gospel at any time there is a meeting going on. The days of the early church where the doors had to be locked because they were conducting secret meetings are over.

Having the doors of the church open during services is not necessarily a strict violation of security parameters when other proactive measures are implemented as well. "And the Lord commended the unjust steward, because he had done wisely: for the children of this world are in their generation wiser than the children of light (Luke 16:8).

When we look at other large special events or gatherings put on in secular arenas, there are security measures and implementations that are always put in place. These events all have certain things in common with church meetings. They all have a large gathering of people of all ages, money is exchanged and there is some type of message, whether in the form of songs by an entertainer, athletes exhibiting their prowess etc.

In a general sense, a church service is a special event as well yet have we been warned by the Gospel that the children of the world are wiser than the children of the light? Why is that? Do we automatically fall back on faith and believe that God has us protected or is it safe to say that because of faith we fail to be wiser?

In my experience as a protection and security advisor and consultant for over forty years, I have been contracted to support various and sundry types of events. These include, but are not limited to, high profile, high net-worth meetings such as shareholder meetings of Fortune 100 through 500 companies, global tours of various entertainers, major brand pushes as well as protection of world class athletes.

Many of the CEO's that head these corporations are staunch believers in the faith, yet they place a premium on security for themselves, families and their companies.

During the shareholder meetings, a special emphasis is placed on the security of the event because the doors are wide open to all shareholders. These attendees have a vested interest in the company and its success. The amount of security used for the event could easily mirror a Presidential visit.

These shareholder meetings occur once a year and the location is moved around the country for two reasons. First, it allows shareholders of different regions the opportunity to attend without having to travel and, secondly, this alleviates having shareholders in their corporate offices.

The security measures implemented are simple and most importantly, cost effective considering how elevated tempers can get. Some of these same measures are easily implemented in the house of faith utilizing its existing church personnel and members.

The Bible was right when it said "And a Child shall lead them". Events like Columbine High, Virginia Tech and Sandy Hook Elementary School have caused experts to take a second look at access to weapons, police response methods and finally school security.

The reaction to the Columbine incident was focused primarily on the response of Law Enforcement and the amount of time it takes for first responders to enter a building and deal with an active shooter. The after action of Virginia Tech's incident focused on reporting methods to the student and administrative bodies and proper coordination of first responders. Little to no attention was put into the overall security measures of either of the schools.

Sandy Hook Elementary wiped the slate clean and focused on the mental health issues in society and weapons again. The children of Sandy Hook put security on the headlines of every news outlet and newspapers all over the country. The Sandy Hook school had security measures in place, however, all it took was one slip in procedure, and the rest is an unfortunate blemish in our society.

An attack on innocent children in a school is a violation of everything we hold sacred as both Americans and humans. Shouldn't we view the church in the same way, as being sacred with an unwritten rule that it is to remain that way? We would all agree with a resounding - yes. I think we would also agree that, in most cases, there are already some security measures implemented in our Houses of Worship, but would we all agree that there are enough?

Now you may ask, "What are we protecting?" The answer is, the same thing that any Fortune 100 company, any school or university would protect: most importantly, people, then property and information.

Fundamentally, we have to structure measures that would protect the church and the church body from *intentional harm, unintentional harm* and *embarrassment*. Let me explain:

Intentional Harm: Premeditated attack [physical harm to person, place or things. Intentional harm is the lack of proper measures or failure to perform those measures that would cause injury loss or damage.

Unintentional Harm: An example of unintentional harm or unintended harm to the church would be leaving personal information in an unsecured location that someone could see.

Embarrassment: Lack of proper security measures that could embarrass the church and give it a bad name in the community.

In an elementary school, each teacher and office staff member represents a security person deputized to perform simple measures. When all are performing their simple tasks you formulate a protective human intelligence gathering fortress, working for one common cause – the safety of the children.

Historically, schools have been a safe haven for children for the 6-8 hours they were there. If we take that concept and transfer it to the House of Worship, we can simply increase security measures at a minimal to no financial cost. Making the church safer can be accomplished without dipping into the church funds in any major way.

Several years ago when I submitted a proposal to a local mega-church to provide executive protection for their pastor I was asked to meet with two deacons to discuss my proposal. We spoke for about an hour, but they never asked me one question about security methodologies, or what, if anything, I needed from them. It was then that I knew that I had to start slow with them in order for them to grasp the concepts I would implement. Security has been a long ignored tool in the American Church, but needs to change with the times.

When I sat down with the pastor, I explained to him that in order to protect him effectively, I had to assess the church's existing security standards. He was receptive but assured me that his church was safe.

I won't elaborate on the findings of my assessment. However, when he read my recommendations he was astonished at how wide open his church was to harm should the wrong person decide to cause a problem. I reassured him that I was not reinventing the wheel, but improving upon his existing protocols.

It is important to stress that point here. This book is not intended to discount what you are doing now, but to build upon that foundation to make your church a harder target, that is seen as less desirable to the wolves of the world.

Each of those measures will be broached in this book so that every, church leader and member can feel more empowered and safer in their own House of Worship.

It was the Apostle Paul who said, "We walk by faith and not by sight" (2 Cor. 5:7). I understand the meaning of this scripture as it puts the emphasis on God's word being the roadmap in our life. By having Faith in His words, we will live a more bountiful and righteous life becoming more like Christ. However, to walk by faith does not mean that we are not to use good sound wisdom when available to us whether in security, or in any other area of our lives.

God gave us the power to both think and discern. In doing so, I believe He wants us to walk by sight when the road has been made clear. If He didn't mean so, He wouldn't have given us our five senses to help us navigate this life with all its pitfalls.

In closing this chapter there will be many strategies given, most of which are simple to implement, to better secure your church building and people.

All these methods will be with the idea of Jesus telling us to be harmless without being victims. We believe you will find it exciting and challenging to see how easy it is to make your building and church family safer and more secure.

When we send our children off to school or loved ones into the public arena, we expect safety issues to be in place for them. Why should we expect any less from the kingdom? While accidents will still happen and bad things will still be a part of life, being prepared to the best of our ability combined with the help and wisdom of God will greatly reduce our liability and risk.

While faith is the only thing that pleases God and by it we procure all His promises, it is by good godly wisdom we navigate many of life's twists and turns. By implementing good security measures when possible is good godly wisdom.

CHAPTER THREE
WHO'S THAT KNOCKING AT MY DOOR - WOLF OR SHEEP DOG?

It is a fact, that the only person mentioning wolves in the four gospels is Jesus. The Pharisees didn't mention wolves. The town's people didn't mention wolves. Even the disciples didn't mention wolves. Sadly, the fact that Jesus had to talk about wolves tells us a few things about both life in the Kingdom as well as life in this world.

Wolves, like every animal, come in different types and varieties. To name a few, there are *political wolves* that feed off those who buy into the lies and rhetoric of politics. There are *legal wolves* who hide behind the law as well as break laws at will to accomplish their agenda. There are even wolves whose goal is to *attack and destroy marriages and families*.

The types of wolves we will be dealing with in this book are those who prey on churches and God-fearing people, because in many ways they are easy targets. Unlocked doors, friendly, trusting, and preoccupied people often make soft targets. This my friend, is my church and yours.

When you think of a wolf there are not many nice things you can say about them. Even in the nursery rhyme *Little Red Riding Hood,* the big bad wolf is portrayed as a deceptive and cunning killer, looking for dinner, which by the way is not much different than the way Jesus portrayed them. The animal kingdom like the human race is filled with all types of personalities: some good and some bad, all different.

Wolves are hunters by nature and nature was kind enough to gift them with all the right tools to get the job done. The wolf, while not spoken of very kindly, is spoken of very consistently. He is a predator par excellence and his favorite food is the food that puts up the least fight. Not much different than the schoolyard bully, the wolf goes for the easy mark. That food is sometimes the peaceful and clueless sheep.

While there is a time to die for your faith and beliefs, it's not something that we usually go out of our way to do. Why, because God also put a particular gift set in us, the gift of self-preservation. While man may be the smartest of all God's creatures he is far from the strongest. In fact we may be one of the most vulnerable of God's creatures

During the Black Plague, something as insignificant and small as an infected flea, put millions of people to death. It was said about the plague, "you had lunch with your family and dinner with your ancestors".

However, God has given us two things that have kept humanity alive and well throughout the ages, despite the incredible obstacles we endured. They are an incredible brain, and a natural born instinct to protect ourselves and those we love.

Let's look at the two basic things that Jesus said about wolves. First, He said that wolves would be cunning and deceptive. Wolves would dress in sheep's clothing to deceive the sheep and take advantage of them. Their attacks would be subtle, surprising and deadly.

Now it is important to note that while the references to wolves made by Jesus mostly described the spiritual danger they would cause, it is quite easy to see that Jesus also implied wolves could be physically dangerous, looking to cause physical harm to God's servants and His people. As we have stated before, persecution for one's faith is one thing, criminal activity is another.

As we look a little further into the makeup of wolves we see that they are very dangerous to sheep. They are sheep's natural enemies. One of the reasons is because wolves are carnivores and sheep are dinner, with no real protective weapons.

When Jesus said I send you out as sheep among wolves, he was saying that there was a good chance that at times our lives would be in danger, and in reality He was okay with that. Perhaps the most obvious thing about sheep is that they are an animal that must be led and protected at times, even from themselves.

One of the things we will talk about later in this book is that among the sheep there are sheep dogs, called to protect the sheep from such harm and danger.

What we really need in the church is a new mindset; one that allows us to truly understand the heart of Jesus. The heart of Christ is not that we become hunters or aggressors, but wise as serpents and harmless as doves. We are called to do as much as we can to protect ourselves, and then leave the rest in God's hands.

You might be saying, "I have not had church security in twenty years and nothing has ever happened." For that, we say, "Praise God!" He is our ultimate protector but that does not remove our responsibility to do our part. He is also our protector when we wear seat belts, life jackets, bike helmets and many other things we do to protect ourselves.

Because the church is an embassy in a hostile territory it is wise to protect its borders as well as its people. As our culture becomes more and more broken and violent, with less and less respect for the laws of God and the land, churches will more and more likely become targets.

When the church takes an unpopular stand on divorce, abortion or other political hot potatoes, wisdom tells us to be watchful. Whenever you take a stand for any principle you will quickly find out who are those against you.

In 1st Corinthians 16:13, Paul tell us to watch, stand fast in the faith, be brave, and be strong. Let all that you do be done in love". The object of church security is not to become hunters of wolves, but to be aware of them and not become their meal.

We are called to be watchful strong, and to walk in love. This can be done in a proactive but loving way. Whether it is a mass shooting, vandalism or child abuse, measures could and should be taken to do our best to protect both the sheep and the shepherds from harm. It is the combination of watching and praying that will give a church a strong security team and presence in its community.

There are three types of harm that we will be talking about throughout this book, most which are highly preventable with some due diligence and watchfulness. The first type of harm and perhaps the most dangerous is *intentional harm*. Intentional harm is when someone has it in their heart to do harm to either the shepherd or any member of the congregation for any reason whatsoever. Whether it is a personal, political or spiritual vendetta their sole purpose is to do harm and bring vengeance or violence.

The second type of harm we mentioned in this book is *unintentional harm*. Unintentional harm can be equally as dangerous, but is not pre-planned, nor does evil necessarily lie at the root of the problem.

The final type of harm we will be talking about is *simple embarrassment.* The reputation of many churches can be easily damaged in a community when someone inadvertently does something that looks bad, and word gets out. Once a church gets a mark against its name it could take years for it to be forgotten. So, whether it is *intentional, unintentional* or *embarrassing*, the idea of the church security team is to limit as best as possible all three scenarios from bringing harm to the sheep, the shepherd, or to the name of the church.

In the next chapter we will give examples of all three types of harm and how a competent church security team can help alleviate the dangers they present.

The Bible gives us parables as great metaphors, analogies and comparative examples that we can use for our lives. The best way to symbolize the importance of this book on church safety is to do the same.

Think of the majority of the church attendees as sheep. They flock together for church meetings with no intention to do each other any harm. Their intent is to fellowship together with their shepherd (their pastor) to worship God, and to hear the Words of Life to take them back to their normal lifestyles.

Sheep are carefree and live their lives with the belief that the shepherd is their safety net, and in many cases, that they cannot be singled out of the flock because there is strength in numbers.

That mindset is tricky. However, because multitudes of sheep have the same thought process, then the entire flock is vulnerable. Most of the time, sheep are in denial and denial can be deadly.

It has been said that denial kills you twice; it kills you once, at your moment of truth, when you are not physically prepared. Denial then kills you a second time because even if you physically survive, you are psychologically scarred by fear, helplessness and horror at your moment of truth.

The good news is that God has also given us sheepdogs. The irony is that the sheep are actually afraid of the sheepdog and try to stay away from him because he resembles more the wolf, than the sheep. The sheepdog by nature is wired to protect the sheep and to deal with the wolf. They avoid him until there is a confrontation with the wolf. At that point the entire flock gets behind the sheepdog, and expects him to protect them.

The analogy is the same with people. Most are comfortable with the recommendations on locking their homes, their cars, and lockers etc. However, they are often adverse to security recommendations when it comes to their house of worship. They feel that extra precautions are not necessary because they are in the house of God or until the wolf appears. Then they seek out the sheepdog that they've avoided. This is the paradox of sheepdogs and sheep.

The presence of the sheepdog is the constant reminder that there are wolves, and this disturbs the sheep. The sheep never think that the wolf will come, but the sheepdog lives for that day. He is trained and gifted for that moment, and knows how to respond appropriately. Although the sheep are not necessarily trained to respond to the wolf, they have an instinctual capacity to look for the sheepdog when the wolf presents itself.

There is an inseparable relationship between the shepherd, the sheep, and the sheepdog. The shepherd leads, feeds, and protects the sheep. He plays a critical role in the lives of the sheep, but he recognizes that he cannot do it alone. Enter his help – the sheepdog. Just as the shepherd teaches and feeds the sheep, he must do the same with the sheepdog.

The shepherd and the sheepdog must be on the same page. They must work in unison, where the shepherd understands the sheepdog's natural capabilities, and the sheepdog knows the shepherd's expectations. This is a vital team dynamic. The sheepdog does not work under his own agenda, but that of the shepherd. He does not wander off on his own, but rather accepts the authority of the shepherd and alerts the shepherd of impending danger when it presents itself. Together they protect the flock; separately they are each at a disadvantage.

Unfortunately, many houses of worship are not keen to having trained security or police officers around until something happens. Then they anxiously await their arrival. That's not how the sheepdog works. Sheepdogs are protectors and preventers by nature.

Law enforcement will diligently investigate the incident *after it has occurred*, but wouldn't it have been better to have the sheepdog present to thwart the event *before it took place*? Sheepdogs need to be with the flock. They are very comfortable with the flock because sheepdogs are sheep that have been given by God the giftset to be sheepdogs.

There is only one special trait that the sheepdog has over the shepherd or the sheep, and that is his ability to take action, and survive in those situations where most sheep cannot. The wolf is a predatory animal that focuses his attention to defenseless animals that are easy targets. They target when there is a need to feed, and they decide when that is going to happen. The well-trained sheepdog and team dynamic with the shepherd can force the wolf to move on to the next flock where there is little to no protection, as we described earlier.

Edmund Burke said, "There is no safety for honest men except by believing all possible evil of evil men". Most of us believe that being a shepherd is a calling. The sheepdog understands the mindset of the sheep and the tactics of the wolf. We believe that real sheep are born that way and that others choose to be sheep-like. We strongly believe that in some sheep resides the potential to be a sheepdog. If you take the average mother who nurtures her child and then place her in a situation where she feels her child is in danger, then watch the sheepdog like response in her. She did not get trained in a school to do that, it is an instinctual response.

That is a shift in mindset. Just as some sheep can recognize the wolf during the attack sequence, there is a significant level or awareness by this select few over the rest of the flock. Herein lies the group that if trained properly, can exponentially fortify the safety of the church.

They however must choose to be converted [trained] to be the sheepdog, and to face the wolf, rather than fall back to the protection of the shepherd and the natural sheepdog. This process can be done with little to no financial investment. The only investment is commitment and time to be properly trained.

We cannot change the wolf, its breed or their need to hunt. Even in those cases where people raise wolves as pets from a pup, you cannot change the genetic makeup of what they are capable of doing. When placing that domesticated wolf amongst the sheep they still need to be watched by the sheepdog that will instinctively pick up on attack behaviors.

This is also the same for the church. Like it or not, there are domesticated wolves that are trying to change their behavior so as to present themselves as "Wolves in sheep's clothing". Remember, this is nothing new. Jesus said it over two thousand years ago, and nothing has changed.

Sadly we can no longer live in the denial that no one would harm someone in church. It is time to identify and train the sheepdogs, which is the aim of this book. Fasten your seatbelts as we begin the adventure of serving as protectors in the house of God.

CHAPTER FOUR
NEW TIMES REQUIRE A NEW MINDSET

So we have discussed why security and safety in a church is a good thing as well as a God thing. We have talked about what the Bible says about protection and how even Jesus Himself understood the need of protection at times.

Why is it however, after decades of churches being considered sacred and places of understood protection are we writing a book on protecting your church? Because it is a new day, a new culture and our world as we know it is not what it used to be.

We are living in a Post-Christian America. Many Christians don't believe that and got mad when President Obama said that we are not a Christian nation. When you consider that one of the top exports of America is pornography and shows like Jerry Springer get aired all over the world from America, you have to wonder if perhaps our president may have a very strong argument.

The real truth is that there are many people who do not feel the same way about Church and houses of worship as we do and many who blame churches for their problems even the problems of our country.

When the government took the Bible and prayer out of Public schools, they created a huge vacuum that had to be replaced with guards and guns. They laid a new foundation for our young people where they would no longer have a basic understanding or respect for the things of God and His people.

Children today do not have the benefit of having school prayer, or learning the Ten Commandments. Their foundation is void of many of the values instilled in the great generations of the forties and fifties and even sixties. Because of these and many other subtle and some not so subtle cultural changes, the church no longer carries the authority or place of sacredness that it once did in our society. Yes, we have gone from the Ozzie and Harriet to Ozzie Osbourne, and that my friend is some generation gap!

The need to protect large gatherings of people is becoming more and more imminent. The more people that gather under a roof the more the chance that someone is mad at one of them.

Schools understand this, colleges understand this, sports and entertainment venues understand this and it is time that the churches catch up with the world on this matter.

Perhaps it is one of the reasons why Jesus said the children of the world are wiser than the children of the Kingdom. Actually, that in some ways can be considered a compliment because we are not to be so familiar with the ways of the world because they are not our ways.

However the Bible also tells us to know our enemy and not be ignorant of his devices. Again the purpose of Church security is not to fight back, but to avoid having to fight by taking simple and fairly inexpensive security measures.

Decades ago, Churches used to be tight knit families of believers who were known throughout their community and respected for their beliefs. There was very little if any crime and when if there was it was usually relatively minor and it was handled internally. Church used to be the place you sat with your mom and dad and maybe even your grandparents. With the divorce rate in America being over fifty percent, however, churches are now being filled with hurting, broken and fractured families, broken people and broken hearts. This is not necessarily a bad thing. In fact, I cannot think of a better place for the broken to gather to come and be restored and healed.

However, while people are busy trying to get their lives back together in the Church, it must be a place that is safe; a place where people can take their mind off self-preservation and put it on knowing God and helping one another.

While sometimes it may seem uncomfortable to talk about safety and security in our churches, there are really some great advantages besides the obvious to have a church safety and security team.

The obvious advantage is that your church building its people and its pastor will now be better protected and people will feel more at ease as they go about doing what God has called them to do. A safe place allows you to be more open and enables you to work on those areas of your life you may not otherwise be willing to show in a public setting.

Some of the other advantages may not be as obvious. Sitting in the chairs of every church, are people who desire to serve God in some capacity and church safety and security is just another opportunity to put them to work.

It provides another ministry to be involved in and make a difference. This goes especially for many men who feel being a Sunday School teacher or singing in the choir is not their cup of tea

From a pastoral point of view, when people are involved in some type of church activity, they tend to more quickly become part of that organization than those who sit and watch what is happening around them. This is good for church growth.

When people work together toward a common goal, such as church safety or security, they feel like they are part of the solution, which makes them feel like they are more part of the church family. Add to this the fact that when people work together on any project or ministry, they get to know each other and form relationships quicker. This is one of the main reasons people stay in, or leave a church.

Another great advantage of a safety and security team is that your visitors will immediately feel more secure when they are noticed and greeted from the time they step on church property.

In a world that has grown so cold and impersonal where often time's people feel like they are treated like numbers, they will take comfort in knowing that the church is diligent in doing their best to make their worship experience both a spiritual one, a safe one and even a personal one.

While no place on this side of Heaven can be called a totally safe place, there are many things we can do to help make our places of Worship safer. A place we are not afraid to bring our family, friends and loved ones.

What it comes down to, is church safety is everyone's job. Whether it's a trip or a fall, a fire, or something leaning more toward a criminal act, we can all have eyes to see and ears to hear. It is sometimes known as the ministry of eyes and ears… the key is knowing what to look for and what to listen for.

You don't need a degree in criminal justice to see if a child is lost or there is an unusual looking person hanging out near the Sunday School rooms. Church safety can be something everyone takes part in and that gives ownership to the people who walk onto your property and through the doors of your church.

In this book you will read security specific methods that are used at the highest levels of government and private industry by security experts and professionals. All of our recommendations are based on these principles. There is no cookie cutter application for every church, office, school, Etc. but the principles can apply to all of these types of venues.

In reading these recommendations we hope to change the mindset and somewhat antiquated belief of what security is and is not. The findings of that assessment should conclude in common sense applications to build upon your existing security measures.

Anyone that tells you that they can implement safety measures for your edifice without performing a complete Risk, Threat, and Vulnerability Assessment (RTVA) is not being honest with you and will place you in a false sense of security [no play on words].

A thorough RTVA will assess your structure, and existing building safety features. They will observe and assess your daily business activities and note all possible risks and vulnerabilities. Additionally, they will observe and assess your church before, during and after worship services. This will include, but is not limited to congregation arrival and departure, offering procedures, or additional services that take place during this time.

At the conclusion of the RTVA they will submit a written report and go over the findings. A truly expert provider will make their recommendations using your pre-existing security measures as a foundation of their recommended security plan.

A large majority of churches have no security measures. There are too many fraudulent companies in existence that will profess to fix your problems with more locks and cameras, however no true RTVA is complete without human interaction and visualization.

Lastly, in the final recommendations there should always be a training recommendation in order to implement the changes.

The security measures that we will recommend will be based off the Concentric Circle Methodology. If you can imagine an outer ring, middle ring and inner ring and overlay that on the church you will be able to understand how to segment your security measures from the:

- **Outer perimeter** secures large zones (church parking lot or sidewalk)
- **Middle perimeter** secures area between the inner and outer rings (church foyer, halls secondary rooms)
- **Inner perimeter** secures the pastor's, leader's and dignitary's immediate area (sanctuary, offices)

The concentric circle principle is the same progressive concept that is used for the White House, United States Capitol and other high profile protected establishments to protect it and those that populate them. The premise of this concept is that security measures are progressively more defined as you move towards the inner circle. The key to making this work is a staff that is trained to be security aware.

In most cases we are not talking about having sentries posted at every corridor and door of the house of worship, but the strategic implementation of reasonable and effective policies. A well-organized security structure is a strong deterrent against many threats.

In the upcoming chapters, this book will address each area of concern specifically, with recommendations that will afford you the proper mindset to adjust where needed.

In the security industry a proactive mindset is key. You don't want to have to clean up a mess you want to keep it from being made. To that end it is important that our recommendations are not just to instruct on *how*, but more importantly on *why*.

When you know *why*, you are able to adjust on the fly and still be effective. For instance, there should be a parking lot ministry that is responsible for safeguarding people upon their arrival and departure. Any areas of isolated parking can be an area of concern and risk.

The addition of having someone visibly managing or overseeing the parking lot is a huge deterrent in presence alone. In the Church world we call this the *Ministry of Presence*. Depending on how many personnel you are able to assign to church security, the parking lot ministry can do frequent "patrols" in the corridors of the church once the service has started.

From our past experience with churches this simple integration makes a difference. We need to always be in the mindset that we have to safeguard all aspects of the church from arrival to departure and church safety starts on the parking lot or the outer perimeter of the church if there is no parking lot.

The often-overlooked parking lot is an extension of your edifice and parishioners have an expectation that their property and personal effects are safe while they worship.

No church wants their house of worship to have the label of being an easy place for theft. At those times where services or other church events occur after dark, this change in security procedures is critically important and can do wonders for making your attendees feel safe and even increase attendance.

Especially in bad neighborhoods it is a well-known fact that people stay home at night because of fear. A well-lit personally managed parking lot says we care about your safety.

For many churches proper lighting is a major step in the right direction. Dark places like parking lots are an open invitation for criminal behavior. Lighting has a psychological effect on feeling safe. (John 3:20)

Adequate lighting makes your members feel safer and a less desirable location for criminal activity because of the possibility of being noticed and identified. Proper lighting and a "periodic" patrol check by a member of the parking lot ministry can increase your safety and security tenfold, as well as put the hearts and minds of your people at ease.

A Shift in proper mindset… do you get the idea now? Anyone looking to cause a problem once they pull on your property and see the Ministry of Presence will think twice and move on.

Most, if not all churches already have an Usher and greeter ministry. We will thoroughly go over the proper usage of these ministries and their responsibilities of the middle and inner rings.

Ushers and greeters are trained to perform specific duties each and every minute of the service. Many of their duties are ritualistic in nature but their fundamental purpose is to interact with people in the church.

Metaphorically speaking, your Ushers are the Secret Service of the church without even knowing it…and that's the secret. They know when standing during a service is out of character for that service. They know most, if not all, of the members as well as they can identify a visitor before they sit.

Although untrained insecurity, they are able to identify most people who are exhibiting unusual personal issues or problems because they know what the norm is for that particular church.

In a positive sense Ushers who are serious about their duties, observe every person that they come in contact with. This position in the church cannot be replaced with a security personality but can be fortified with specific security training for the ushers.

Think about how much safer you would feel knowing that your ushers have been trained to recognize *red behavior* and how to effectively handle the situation.

If you implemented our first recommendation with the trained parking lot ministry in conjunction with an usher ministry with a proper proactive security mindset, think about how much more fortified your safety and security would be without any video or technical equipment.

For most churches, that would increase your safety one hundred percent. Understand that these measures are cost effective because you are not hiring a security team, but giving a sense of ownership and servitude to those already working within the church.

We have personally seen and witnessed the satisfaction that members have when they are performing specific duties that are directly associated with the safety of their church. In the previous chapters I mentioned the pastor who hired me to protect the church and him during his campaign for public office.

I trained and got the parking lot ministry and ushers involved in practicing a proactive security mindset and was met with elation from both ministries. We set up monthly security meetings to go over any concerns and always had 100% attendance. These are but just basic common sense, low dollar applications that pays for themselves.

In the upcoming chapters we will recommend more of these simple applications that any house of worship can implement with minimal cost and time.

CHAPTER FIVE
AN EYE FOR AN EYE
THE FORCE CONTINUUM

When people come to church they have many expectations based on their current situations, issues they are dealing with and ultimately their relationship with their God.

Once the service starts there is a fair expectation that no one expects any disruptions and if one occurs, it is safe to say that in most cases, no one is truly prepared nor desires to deal with un-church like behavior in the House of God.

When confronting any disruption or threat of disruption to a church service, the church security team has to follow the same rules that any police officer or any sworn representative of the law would have to. These rules are known as the "Force Continuum".

The Force Continuum is like a sliding scale of escalation from soft to hard confrontation. It is vital to understand how this sliding scale works in order to de-escalate situations and keep yourself and others out of trouble and above the law. It is also important to fully understand this chapter to avoid not only criminal litigation, but civil litigation both to you as well as the church you are serving.

Reasonable Force

Unlike police, the average citizen is *not required nor expected* to ever make an arrest. Under the best circumstances we merely observe, report and call the police if a crime occurs in our presence.

However, if a private citizen ever needs to take someone into custody for a crime, he or she must use reason and common sense. The law varies from state-to-state, but generally allows citizens to make an arrest and use reasonable force in doing so.

One common definition of reasonable force is *not excessive force under the circumstances.* This means to consider the seriousness of the crime, the risk of harm for everyone, and the immediacy of the situation. So if you see someone stealing apples from the local grocery store a Taser™ or baton might get you in more trouble than they. The preference always is to get a law enforcement response to affect the arrest.

While there may have been a time when the church could take care of its own dirty laundry, this is no longer the case in our litigious society. Many crimes today in fact are reportable by law and must not be kept silent.

Level One

Ministry Of Presence: The mere presence of a highly visible usher team is often enough to stop many a disruption in progress or prevent future ones. Included in overall presence is standing, walking, and running. Without saying a word, an alert church representative can deter disruptions or potential issues away from the church property by use of body language and gestures. At this level gestures should be non- threatening and professional. Sometimes called the ministry of presence, this is the first tool used to prevent and avoid negative behavior on church property.

Level Two

Verbal Communication: Sometimes referred to as *verbal judo.* Used in combination with a visible presence, the use of the voice can usually achieve the desired results. Words can be whispered, used normally, or shouted to be effective. The content of the message is as important as your demeanor. It's always best to start out calm, but firm and non-threatening. Choice of words and intensity can be increased as necessary or used in short staccato like commands in serious situations. The right combination of words in combination with Church presence can de-escalate a tense situation rather quickly and prevent the need for a physical altercation.

At this point I should mention that physical altercations should always be avoided as much as possible. Besides the danger to the people fighting there can be collateral damage as well as legal retribution brought on by the person intending to cause harm or disruption. At times the person causing the problem may actually try to lure your ushers/security team into a physical altercation so that they can bring a lawsuit against the church. Training and experience improves the ability of the church representative to communicate effectively with everyone, including the police and know what response is called for in case a situation arises.

Level Three

Assuming the first two measures have failed, the next level of response is: *Control Holds & Restraints*: Certain situations may arise where words alone do not reduce the aggression in an individual. Sometimes you will need to get involved physically. At this level, minimal force would involve the use of bare hands to guide, hold, and restrain. This does not include offensive moves such as punching, tackling, and choking. *Pain compliance holds* could apply here, but only after ordinary holds fail to control an aggressive individual. From this point on, it is our recommendation that only specially trained security individuals deal with the end of the force continuum where a baton or similar defensive instruments may be used.

At this level a baton may be used as a self-defense mechanism to block blows or temporarily restrain a suspect. Handcuffs may also be used as a restraint devise only if the person has been trained to do so.

Most individuals do not need to be handcuffed. They should only be used on a person who exhibits aggression, poses a real threat or where flight is a real possibility. Handcuffs should not be applied too tightly and should be double-locked when safe to do so. Once a suspect is handcuffed, the person applying them is responsible to see that they don't trip or fall. It is also important not to pile on top or place the handcuffed suspect face down on the ground to avoid "positional asphyxiation". Hog-ties should **not** be used by security Specialists.

Level Four

Chemical Agents: **While we** *do not suggest the use of chemical agents in the church; however, it is important for you to understand how the force continuum works.* Sometimes when the suspect is violent or threatening, more extreme, but non-deadly measures must be used in defense to bring the suspect under control or affect an arrest. Before moving to level four, it is assumed that other less physical measures had been tried and deemed inappropriate.

When used by surprise, pepper spray and tear gas is an excellent distraction, allowing the security Specialist time to get away, call the police, or subdue the suspect.

Contrary to media advertising, pepper spray does not have stopping power or cause paralysis. An assailant can still grab you, punch you, stab you, or shoot you and will definitely be angrier after being sprayed. Also, tear gas may not be effective on the insane, addicted, intoxicated or hysterical persons.

Tear gases (CN, CS, and OC) can be handheld, hand-thrown, or propelled. Security Specialist's usually only get involved with handheld canisters containing pepper spray. Pepper spray should not be used to protect property or to enforce business rules. Remember, it's a defensive weapon.

Pepper sprays need to be directed in the suspect's face for maximum result and not sprayed wildly at groups of people. Even though considered non-deadly, chemical sprays can cause a severe reaction and even death to a suspect with medical or allergic conditions.

Also, pepper sprays have a blinding effect and care must be used that spray victims do not fall down stairs or walk into traffic or operate motor vehicles.

Level Five

Temporary Incapacitation: To use force under level five means that the situation was so extreme, violent, and immediate that it was necessary to temporarily incapacitate a suspect prior to arrival of the police. This includes the use of all methods of non-deadly force beginning with the empty hand up through and including impact tools such as a baton. At level five, properly used defensive and offensive moves are allowed under the right circumstances.

Choke holds and carotid neck holds can be used, but at great risk. Although still taught at many police academies, neck compressions are very risky and used only in extreme situations. Baton blows to the suspect's head or throat can be deadly and inconsistent with professional training standards.

Temporary incapacitation is used to stop a suspect from injuring you or others long enough to handcuff and restrain them. Baton blows to soft tissue and certain joint areas are all consistent with professional security training standards.

As a general rule stun guns are part of level five, but should not be used by security specialists except on special posts and only by those authorized and trained in the use and effects of the device. Stun guns are handheld devices and some like the Air-Taser propel charged darts on leads at a suspect.

Level Six

Deadly Force: Deadly force should only be used when you are in immediate fear of death or great bodily injury at the hands of a perpetrator. It is only then that you are authorized to use deadly force in most states.

Check your state laws to be sure. Deadly force can be applied with your hands, impact tools, or with a firearm.

There are no rules, other than negligence, for applying deadly force when it's justified. However, deadly force is the highest standard and must be justified. This force continuum will be considered in the aftermath as a test to see if other alternatives were used first or were more appropriate.

For everyone, the use of the firearm is the most troublesome because of the range of the bullet. You may be justified is shooting an assailant standing in front of you, but not justified for wounding innocent bystanders. Similarly, you may have been justified in shooting a person charging at you with a knife, but not justified after he turns to run away.

Handguns should never be pulled and brandished as a deterrent or be used as a control tool under level three. The use of armed personnel in the church is an extremely difficult decision to make. In many states it is illegal to carry a handgun within the boundaries of church property unless you are a sworn officer or have the explicit permission of the pastor in writing.

That withstanding, it should never be viewed as the solution to all of your problems. Carrying a handgun legally while performing security functions has been a long-standing debate among security professionals.

We are not anti-gun, anti-Second Amendment advocates. However, we are proponents of responsible handgun application. Carrying a handgun is a double-edged sword that assuredly will result in some court proceeding, whether criminal or civil even when justified.

This is why prevention and avoidance is so important in your church security philosophy. So much trouble can be avoided by being alert, knowing what to look for and having people trained for a proper reaction.

CHAPTER SIX
TROUBLE IN THE OUTER LIMITS

In the church world, some people bring their problems to the altar and some come to the altar to cause a problem. This is not a common thing, but you only have to be right once to save your church or ministry a lot of embarrassment, bad press and possible physical harm to those at the altar.

The object of this book is to spot those people who want to cause a problem and either help them to help themselves or keep them from causing harm in your church environment.

As a church we welcome all people who truly want the help of God, however not everyone that walks in the door is a sheep. When the wolf calls the shepherd must have a plan.

In people, trouble works from the inside out. However, when it comes to troubles in the church, it works the opposite. If you are going to have trouble in the church, it has to make its approach from the outside in. Be it by bus, car or foot *all trouble must first walk in the front door.*

Since the vast majority of everyone entering the church building walks in some type of main entrance, you can set your security up in three basic parameters: outside the front door, inside the front door and private office and staff areas.

Breaking your security into layers or rings* (we will explain this further in Chapter 7) enables you to use more people to both see a problem and prevent a problem. That it is why it is important to see the problem as early as possible so that there is time to decide the best way to deal with it in a way that is most efficient and causes the least amount of distraction and or damage. The idea of church safety is always to prevent problems before they happen and not have to call the police afterwards.

The first line of defense is what we would call your parking lot ministry. As we've said earlier in this book, most of the principles for making your church a safer place do not require large amounts of money. Volunteers working together not only keeps your church safe, but gives ownership of your church to those men and women involved in the process.

The parking lot ministry is the first people your guests see when pulling into your church. Whether it is actually in the parking lot or on the sidewalk in front of the main entrance they serve a great purpose besides the one that is most obvious. They not only direct traffic but help people out the cars and get them into the building safely. On rainy days they may provide umbrellas and on icy days a steady hand.

All the while they are carrying out these more basic parts of this ministry, they are doing something no one is really paying attention to… they are paying attention to and observing who is getting out of cars and to anything or anyone that seems out of place.

When and if they spot something that doesn't look right, they are now in a position to do several things. They can get license plate information, engage in conversation to investigate further, radio ahead to next perimeter, or call for law enforcement to further look into the situation.

If they radio ahead to the next perimeter the questionable person or persons can be watched to limit any problem that might occur or they can call for help if necessary. People in the outer perimeter, keep the church from being blindsided by a problem before it gets too close to the church building and those people in it.

Besides the obvious advantage of spotting a problem before it walks into the building, having people in the outer perimeter brings a level of comfort and sense of welcome to those coming to worship the Lord. Especially in this new post Christian culture we live in, this is one of the things that will keep people coming back to a church; a sense of welcome and safety.

Having this ministry will also be a blessing to the people involved as those who get involved in a church stay in a church. It is a win-win situation where everyone is blessed and there is no cost to carry out this process. Only some friendly and willing saints who want to get involved helping make their church a safer place. Workers in this ring need only to be friendly and observant not necessarily strong or tough, although that certainly does not hurt.

In order for any church or facility that participates in the gathering of people and therefore important people to have effective security, they should use the Concentric Circle Methodology of security measures.

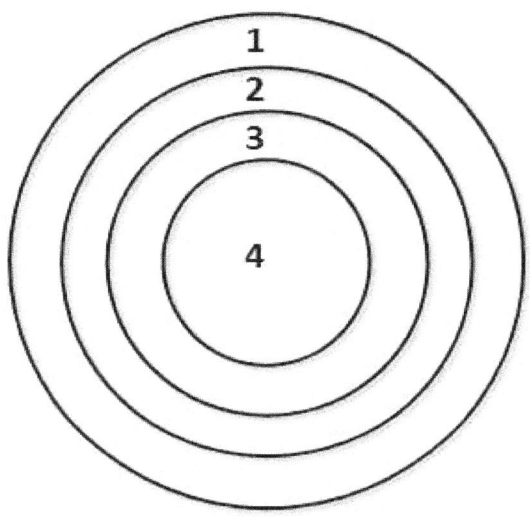

1 – Outer [outside the church]

2 – Middle [Inside the church doors/classrooms, restrooms]

3 – Inner [Congregation- sanctuary]

4 – Pastors, Leaders and Dignitaries

The concentric circle philosophy allows for the screening and observation of all persons succeeding into the next circle, as they get closer to the center. If at any point something unusual is noticed, a person should be assigned to keep an eye on this person. Using *aggressive friendliness* would be a good thing to use at this time.

The Concentric Circle Methodology is used at the highest levels of security because it is effective.

These by the way are the same protocols used to protect the President of the United States and other Heads of State by the United States Secret Service.

This chapter will address the outer ring. When members of your church arrive for meetings they all arrive outside the building and park either in your parking lot, on the street or dropped off outside and walk in. Regardless of how they arrive, they are in the outer ring of your safety responsibility.

The presencee of this outer ring can have a major impact and a comforting effect on your members. More importantly, it provides a deterrent for anyone who may have ill intent. Having a parking lot ministry or presence allows your church personnel to observe moods and behaviors as the members filter into your building.

The outer ring is the first observation point of activity before anyone enters into the building. For the Church this is not a security point where access is limited after a search of anyone, but a point where observation skills are critical.

Anyone assigned to this post is responsible for paying attention to the normal and abnormal behavior of those about to enter the church. For the most part arriving church members have a specific personality and behavior. Most, if not all are cordial. They exchange pleasantries when spoken to and enter with an attitude of respect of the church and the services that are about to take place.

Members who have a heavy heart or are going through personal issues seek comfort as they approach the doors.

Assigning a person or persons that are familiar with church members and can tell the difference when they see them is a key to both bringing comfort to the burdened as well as helping maintain safety in the church.

Assigning a person to work in the outer ring who is somewhat familiar with the church membership allows them to notice visitors or those people who are not regular attendees.

When we audited and observed other church security, we were amazed that the person assigned in the outer ring knew everyone who was entering the church and quickly observed those persons who were visitors and not regular members. One thing they all had in common that we strongly advise, was that they greeted everyone, including the visitors with a warm welcome.

The outer ring for church safety should be seen as a passive security post. What that means is that the church members will not be going through metal detectors or physical search of their personal effects, which sadly takes place in many churches around the country. Speaking to people engages them in an interview that is unknown to them.

A normal exchange of pleasantries is something that you do not have to be trained in to observe if there is a problem. When you say, "Good morning" to someone, it should elicit a specific response, whether verbal or non-verbal. A smile and a nod is the usual response from someone who has something on their mind or someone that is not familiar with the up close and personal personality of the church. Eye contact is another important observation in every aspect of security. Anyone intending on doing harm does everything they can to do one thing – *keep from being noticed.*

Once people are inside the church and the services begin, the outer ring must be maintained. The job is *not* over. The personal property of the church members is vulnerable at this point.

Presence is still critical and important. This presence is a visible showing of deterrence while church activities are taking place. It also sends a message that this is a church that care for you and what is important to you.

Once the services or meeting is over the outer ring is now responsible for observing the church members as they exit the building and leave the property.

Observe and Report is also known as *see something, say something.*

Any "concerning or unusual" behavior that is observed by anyone working the outer circle as people exit the church should be relayed and passed on to the middle and inner rings of the concentric circles to continue the observation. It is within these inner rings that observation skills and interaction is much more critical. We will address those responsibilities in the upcoming chapters on the other rings. We highly recommend that the leadership of the church have a relationship with the local police. I suggest that you meet with the police and let them put you on their daily patrols, especially days of scheduled services or meetings. Having a marked car patrolling the immediate area during the beginning and end of services is another deterrent and reduces response time if needed.

Some churches have established relationships with their local police to have off-duty officers with marked cars on their parking lots. While this may be somewhat of a deterrent, this is an expense that can be alleviated by establishing the aforementioned relationship and having your church added to their daily patrols on services and meeting days.

While it should be noted that anyone bent on committing a crime will probably do so our goal in this book is to turn your church into a hard target that will make a person think twice before causing a problem. The bottom line in the outer circle is to remember that you have the first look at any potential problem that will enter the church and the thing they want most is for you to not notice them.

Being overly friendly to someone like that and looking them in the eye as you greet them, is another way of saying I have you on my radar. That alone will usually make a person think twice. Bottom line, anyone with evil in mind does not want to be noticed!

CHAPTER SEVEN
STUCK IN THE MIDDLE WITH YOU - THE HOLY PLACE

As we said earlier in chapter six, in order for any church or facility that participates in the gathering of people *as well as* important *figures* to have effective security they should use the Concentric Circle Methodology of security measures. – Outer [outside the church, parking lot, sidewalk]

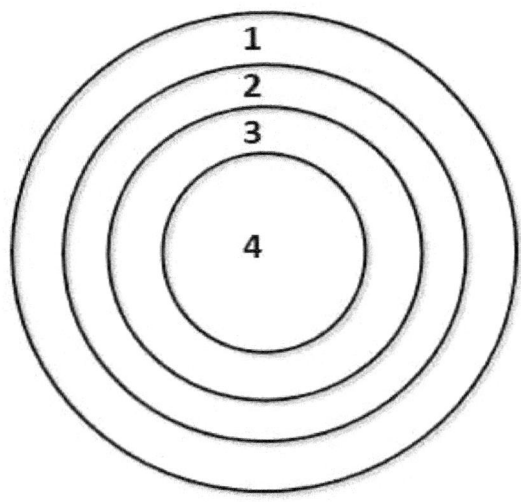

1 – Middle [Inside the church doors/foyer, offices, and classrooms]

2 – Inner [Congregation/Sanctuary]

3 – Pastors, Leaders and Dignitaries

As mentioned earlier, this is the same philosophy of protection used to protect the President of the United States as well as other very high profile figures by the United States Secret Service.

The concentric circle philosophy allows for the screening and observation of all persons *moving from one circle* into the next circle as they get closer to the center.

This Concentric Circle Methodology is used at the highest levels of security because it is *simple but yet* effective.

This chapter will address the middle ring. The middle ring is usually the first point of entry into *the interior of* a venue, building, or in this matter – The Church building. Just because a person has passed your safety measures of the outer ring, it does not mean it is safe to assume that they should be deemed safe.

The second ring would take into consideration all interior areas with the exception of the sanctuary. This ring would include all offices, Sunday School rooms, and nurseries, dining hall, café's, bookstores, shops, overflow rooms, restrooms and various other places. Basically, the middle perimeter would entail any place under the roof with the exception of the sanctuary itself.

Too often security recommendations have focused solely on those who attend the church meeting inside the sanctuary and very little emphasis on the value of other property of the church that also has monetary value and most importantly contain human life.

In those churches that have Sunday Schools or Children Church programs, the children usually gather in a separate location from the main sanctuary, away from those who protect them the most – their parents and loved ones.

Children's Class Rooms

The days of dropping children off at Sunday School and returning to pick them are a thing of the past. There are several inexpensive measures that can be implemented to insure that the adult that left them at the Sunday School is in fact the correct adult to whom the child is released. Your procedures should be simple, resolute and sound when it comes to children.

There should be strict adherence to the policies you set. As a rule, it is good to have fewer rules, but be disciplined in enforcing them, rather than have a lot of rules that are enforced differently by different people. Like everything in life, once something becomes a habit, it is easy to follow whether it is a good one or a bad one. When it comes to the most precious gifts we have, our children, our habits must be excellent.

A good piece of wisdom to remember when it comes to keeping things running smooth, is "don't expect what you don't inspect".

100		100
Pager Number	Child's Name First & Last	
Jesus Loves Children And So Do We!	Parent's Name First & Last	Pager Number
Please fill out the label to the right & place it on your child's back. You must present this stub when you pick up your child. Children are released to parents or guardians only. © churchnursery.com, 2004	Parent's Location During Child's Nursery Stay **Please Check All That Apply:** ☐ Visitor ☐ Bottle @____ ☐ Nursing ☐ Potty Training ☐ Diaper ☐ Diaper Bag ☐ Pacifier ☐ Snacks OK ☐ Medical Alert____ ☐ Allergy Alert____	

Many Proven Design Ideas!

Jesus Loves Children!   **100**

And So Do The People At
Hickory Creek Baptist Church!

Please fill out the label on the other side of this sheet and place it on your child's back. If your child needs you during the worship service, we will activate your pager. Please present this stub when you pick up your child. Children are released to parents or guardians only.

Pager # _____
Keep This Stub Handy!

100

Child's Full Name
Parent's Full Name   Child's Age
Parent's Location During Stay   Pager #

Please Check All That Apply:
- ☐ Snacks OK   ☐ Potty Training   ☐ Diaper Bag   ☐ Pacifier
- ☐ Nursing   ☐ Allergy
- ☐ Bottle/Cup   ☐ Medical Alert
- ☐ Special Instructions

This brings us into the next recommendation. We highly recommend that anyone associated and interacting with the children be required to have a background check conducted to ensure that they are considered safe to be with children.

Oversight in this area is a major mistake for any institution that accommodates children. In fact, many public schools have now implemented the background check procedure to the point that even if a parent is a chaperone for their own child, but has to interact with the children of others on a school trip, or other function, they are also required to have a background check.

For some this may seem as an invasive measure, especially since you may be dealing with "Sister So and So," who you have known for years. However, those who are truly dedicated to that ministry and whose first priority is to protect the children should understand and have no problem having their background checked.

It should be noted, that even with a background check that comes back clean, it is very important to know those who labor among you. It is a fact that a majority of pedophiles don't get caught till they have repeated the act multiple times, therefore knowing a person's character is equally as important as a clean background check.

While this can be a sensitive matter if handled with love and clear explanation, it will weed out many people who otherwise may have applied that might not be able to pass a background check. For that reason alone, it is good to have this as a standard operational procedure.

In the long run this will protect both children and the reputation of any worker that might be suspected of any wrongdoing. Certainly, if someone knows they cannot pass a background check, it would be quite un- likely that they would submit to one. This also saves a lot of time and embarrassment and helps avoid the possibility of having to offend someone by telling them they do not qualify to work with children.

ROOMS

Depending on your budget, Sunday School and childcare program rooms should have security cameras that feed into a quality recording system. Also, it is great to have a monitor that can be watched by the ushers in the event of a problem.

Once again if people know they are cameras present it tends to keep the wrong type of people out of those areas. This also allows you to always have video evidence in the event anything unfortunate happens or perhaps even if someone is falsely accused which is happening more frequently in our litigious culture. In these types of situations, a picture is truly worth a thousand words and often times thousands of dollars.

These rooms should also have windows for both parents and ushers to view what is going on as well as all doors should be able to be locked in the event of an emergency. It is always advisable that all teachers carry a cell phone in class again in case an emergency arises.

Once again, it is important that we take every reasonable precaution to protect the most precious and yet vulnerable resources of the church, its young people. By carrying out these different policies we make the church a harder target and anyone looking for an easy situation to perpetrate evil will move on to a softer target down the road.

The Offices

We cannot address everything you keep in your offices, but suffice it to say, there is equipment [computers, Etc.], as well as confidential financial documents and sensitive information about both church members and staff. There is some type of value that can be placed on all of them. Whether a monetary value or personal information, it is critical that we are diligent to safeguard them from the wrong hands.

Church membership files contain enough information that when in the wrong hands; can put a church member at risk for identity theft, home burglary or even physical harm. These files should be maintained in a locked cabinet within a locked office. Access to these files should be limited to authorized administrative church personnel.

Once again the world has led the way in trying to keep people's privacy protected. The HIPPA Act (Health Insurance Portability and Accountability Act) is a good example of the extremes our Western culture will go to help keep our private lives private. It goes without saying that all computers should be password protected and only those who are trusted employees and or workers in the church that need access should have it.

Open doors with unoccupied offices can breed unwanted curiosity as well as an open invitation to someone intending on doing wrong. Offices should be secured at all times when they are not occupied. Access should be limited to "authorized church personnel" or those members conducting church business only.

Access control should not emulate trying to enter a fortress or be manned by harsh faces, but should be dealt with by intelligent measures balanced with love and grace. This process can be started today and save a lot of trouble tomorrow.

Nurseries

The church nursery is one of the most vulnerable areas of a church and that is because it contains our most vulnerable members, babies. As mentioned before, all nursery workers must be trusted members who have passed a background check. Nursery doors should always have windows on them so that a parent walking by can look in and check on their child. Our personal opinion is that nursery doors should remain locked at all times both for the protection of the children getting out and unwanted visitors getting in.

The nursery should above all be a safe place where a child can roam without fear of being harmed. Look for things that can be pulled off a shelf or other such hazards. Also, it is important to have pre-written policies for the nursery workers to follow. Later on in our legal considerations chapter we will talk about the power of having good policies.

People Power

We made common sense application of human presence on the outer perimeter where your members and visitors have their first interaction with your church's safety and security team. The middle perimeter should exhibit the same presence.

We want to be careful here as we recommend these simple recommendations that they won't appear as sentries guarding the halls. But rather well-meaning and loving people trying to keep a place of worship both a safe and secure environment for the youngest child to the most important adult.

Assigning someone or a group of individuals to periodically walk [patrol] the middle perimeter is a good start for most churches. Having a rotation of patrols, usually ushers in this section will do wonders to help mitigate any breach in church safety and security. This is also most often the most resisted recommendation of all because of a couple factors.

Most institutions erroneously think this means contracting a security service or off-duty law enforcement when it does not. Diligent men and women of the church with some small amount of training can walk around the facility and be the eyes and ears for any situation that needs attention. Some churches have what we call an "Eyes and Ears Team". These people are trained to know what to look for and to report any possible problems to the right people in charge.

Some thoughts regarding this type of ministry are as follows:

1. Church members assigned to this portion of the safety program feel they are not unable to attend the church service, therefore they are often reluctant to participate. Consider offering them a free CD of the service to help alleviate that problem.

2. Proper selection of the right people is difficult if you do not know what experience the person needs.

3. Who trains the church personnel on proper security/safety and reporting procedures

A very important consideration in the middle perimeter aspect is whether the personnel utilized should be selected or accepted on a volunteer basis? We want to share my insight on this very issue because it is a critical one. When it comes to certain areas of church work we believe people should be selected because of their giftedness, not because they volunteer.

Often time people volunteer for things they want to do, not the things they are gifted or trained to do. This causes two problems. The first problem is if you use volunteers you may end up with the wrong people doing the job just because they volunteered.

This is especially true in the church safety and security ministry. What better place for a bad guy to learn the ways of the church than to volunteer to be on the church safety and security team. Choose the people you think have the best natural and spiritual abilities and then train them.

The other problem with volunteers is if you see they clearly can't do the job you have to tell them and this often times will cause embarrassment and hurt feelings even to the point of them leaving the church. Keep in mind, there is just as much strength in using someone who has no security experience, but possesses great people skills, as with someone who has an extensive security background, but poor people skills. *It is very important to understand that the word de- escalation should be the watchword for church safety.*

CHAPTER EIGHT
THE GREAT DISTRACTION

We have touched on the outer and middle circles of the Concentric Circle Methodology. We are now going to speak on the inner most portion of the concentric ring concept. This is where the masses are all gathered in one location for an extended period of time.

From a church gathering perspective, this is the most vulnerable time of the service. It is so very vulnerable for the following two reasons; regardless of whether your church is a large or small church, the inner circle [Sanctuary] is the gathering place for all members and visitors and ministers. It is the one place where the most amount of damage can be done in the shortest amount of time.

Secondly, it is during this time in the sanctuary, people are divinely distracted by the love and presence of God probably feeling safe and wanting to dig further into the Spirit; hence the great distraction. It is the perfect storm for a ship of doom to sail into.

As we said earlier in the book, from a safety and awareness standpoint the Usher team is your first line of defense to notice the person with the red behavior. When I say this, do not envision them as a uniform security force, but rather as your sanctuary behavior experts. The usher team interacts with members and visitors on a regular basis. They know, for the most part, all of the church members and recognize visitors when they attend your services.

Most experienced ushers can recognize the behavioral traits of visitors even by the way they enter the sanctuary. One senior usher of a church that we consulted about security measures told us that she can spot visitors as soon as they walk into the sanctuary. She stated that visitors enter the sanctuary and look around for a place to sit, whereas member tend to sit in the same general area.

She further stated that the sanctuary is territorial in a sense that most members will sit in the same place every church service and other member respect that sacred seating space.

Entire pews have become unwritten family property, and other members will readily tell a visitor, "You can't sit there." This short glimpse into the mindset of just one Usher reiterates my suggestion that the Ushers are your inner perimeter security force.

The visitor behavior is only the fact that obvious due to the fact that ushers know the order of service and how the congregation should be responding. During times such as praise and worship or prayer and reflection there is a specific behavior consistent with this moment in time. An experienced usher recognizes inconsistent behavior. Is this a sign of danger?

No, but it is time for that internal alarm to go off. Inconsistent behaviors throughout the evolution of the service could signal the need for closer attention or intervention.

In my experiences visiting churches I closely watch the ushers throughout a service. They are very regimented in what they do and when they do it. In many cases they come across almost like a silent drill team or synchronized element.

There is no wasted energy. This behavior from the perspective of a member or visitor garners a level of respect. Ushers are some of the most visible church staff during church gatherings. Their expertise in the order of the church gathering is priceless. In their process of performing their duties they are unknowingly providing a safe environment. When an Usher is properly trained their knowledge can be fine-tuned into a formidable proactive force.

In my experience with consulting church security I have found that the ushers readily accept this added responsibility. In most of the cases they feel that it was their implied duties already.

There is a perfect synergy between existing responsebilities and refined proactive measures. The transition between being your standard well-trained usher to an usher with a proactive protection mindset is not as difficult as it sounds.

Ushers are a similar equivalent to the close protection that you see with the President of the United States. Each individual is highly trained to address every problem. Having that sense of security within the church gives your members added comfort because it will be noticeable.

Addressing responses to many potential problems in the church can be set in place so that if any problem escalates the proper response is made without having to waste any time.

As we mentioned in Chapter 5, the response to any given situation must be consistent with the issue and if not trained properly a wrong response can escalate your problem to an unnecessary level and put your church at risk.

This is the importance of training. We are not implying that your ushers need to be the equivalent to a Special Forces church unit; however, we do feel that they should be a church unit with special training.

We have witnessed a clear difference in how the ushers perform their duties after they have been trained in proactive measures. They tend to speak more to people and to analyze their response behavior, as well as more observant of the entire sanctuary.

Well trained ushers are a priceless commodity in the whole scheme of church protection.

Depending on the order of the church services your ushers can be easily trained to add a more protective value to specific times such as offerings or when the shepherd leaves the pulpit and interacts within the congregation.

This chapter is not aimed at offering protective training or instruction, but rather to open your mind to options that are available to maximize your existing personnel. There are qualified experts in the protection industry who can teach these protocols, and drill the information until it becomes second nature and automatic. The importance of training is to work at things not just till you get them right, but till you can't get them wrong.

The pastor or preacher is the leader of the house of worship. He or she is a lightning rod for things both good and bad. Along with that responsibility will come both adoration, accolades as well frustration, jealousy and even anger.

Protecting the leader of the house of worship is a very important, yet specific task. It has to be done in a way that does not make the members feel that he or she is not being kept away from their pastor yet done in a manner that makes him or her not physically accessible to inflict harm.

Proper training is highly recommended in larger churches where there is a security team assigned to protect the pastor. Specific assignments and positions are installed to provide a protective bubble to the pastor to allow him/her to move freely within the house of worship yet have some form of protection.

In smaller churches where there is not a specific team assigned to provide this protection there should be training incorporated that incorporates the staff that is working each church service.

One of the ways to carry out this option is by assigning specific zones within the inner perimeter or sanctuary where a staff member is responsible for the pastor's safety in that area. This option allows the pastor to move freely without the distraction of having a security team moving with them.

Especially for church work, this is a much more laid back form of security where people may not feel that their pastor is walking around with high powered security yet He is being watched over at all times.

High profile guests often visit churches to worship. Many of these high profile guests do not have their own personal security and others do not travel with their own protection team. Their safety and security becomes the responsibility of your church.

As stated before, in larger churches where there is a designated security ministry, a person or persons who are assigned to high profile guests during their visit. They are to provide safety and security of that high profile guest and should not have any responsibility to care for the pastor during the service[s]. In smaller churches, where there is no security ministry per se, you still want to incorporate some safety and security measures for them as a courtesy.

It is better to assign an usher or other church staffer who is properly trained as we recommend to be assigned to them during their visit. This person is sole responsibility is to the guest and not to respond to any unforeseen issue occurs.

The reason that we encourage this specific assignment in both large and small churches is that case studies have shown that most, if not all attacks occur with the use of some diversion. In the midst of this diversion if there is no clear understanding of responsibility it is easy to have your attention distracted momentarily and not perform as expected.

When the staffer completely understands who they are responsible for, and know that the other staffers are properly trained and will conduct themselves appropriately, they will not hesitate to respond properly. Simple following orders will keep everyone in their land and that will help eliminate any attacks by use of diversion.

The inner ring of the concentric ring concept is the most vulnerable place in safety and security. The inner ring depends on the outer and middle rings to perform effectively and Whatever can get past the outer and middle ring now becomes the problem of the inner ring which as we have stated is the most vulnerable ring of all.

A key component to make the concentric circle method work is communications between the rings. If a red behavior is spotted in the outer ring and not reported, it is as good as not being spotted.

Good security is a team effort. Communications and interactions between the team members and the rings mean fewer surprises' and quicker dealing with any situations that may arise that in turn means better safety and security for both your church family and any guests that may be visitors.

CHAPTER NINE
RECOMMENDATIONS AND LEGAL CONSIDERATIONS

It goes without saying that there are legal considerations when operating as a church. Whether it's how you keep books, do counseling or in this case run your safety and security team there are some things that must be considered.

Some of the basic considerations such as incorporating your church and keeping excellent corporate records go without saying, however, there are many churches that operate without the basic legal considerations for their protection.

When it comes to your church's security, you should always focus your goals on mitigating intentional harm, unintentional harm, and embarrassment. We addressed the first two in the preceding chapters of this book. However, embarrassment can also affect the church, its members and its ability to continue to operate after unforeseen occurrences.

Embarrassment can turn your members away from your house of worship and affect your weekly, attendance, finances and operations.

In 2010 a very prominent Bishop this country was accused in a lawsuit by multiple young men of abusing his spiritual authority by lavishing them with gifts with the purpose of coercing them into sexual acts during overnight trips. The case was settled out of court in 2011.

However, because of this being an embarrassment as well as an immoral incident, the church suffered from a departure of one of its prominent Elders. This departure prompted a large number of members to depart as well. The church took a huge financial downturn and started reducing many of its daily operations to handle the burden. This in many ways is ALL due to the embarrassment.

There is a certain expectation of safety when people come to your house of worship, and it is your responsibility to do your best to see that their expectations are met.

Along with every recommendation, we have made in this book thus far we would be remiss if we overlook or dismiss proper licensing and certifications in those specific areas that are regulated by some local, state or federal governing body. This book was specifically aimed and written to guide you to view the safety and security of the house of worship as a necessity rather than scare into building a fortress.

In 2001, *Christian Today* listed the top ten lawsuits churches were exposed to at that time: [Not listed in any particular order] please note that although there may be numerous areas in which churches may be in danger of being sued, this is certainly a good place to start.

1. Suits based on negligence—general public.
2. Suits based on negligence—parishioners.
3. Suits based on negligence—"nuisance events" that attract young adults.
4. Suits based on negligence—supervision of employees.
5. Suits based on sexual harassment.
6. Suits based on defamation.
7. Suits based on apparent authority.
8. Suits based on disputes over election of the pastor.
9. Suits based on disclosure of confidential information.
10. Suits based on unfair acts.

In one case, a woman in Michigan sued her church of 12 years because in a church service she responded to the altar call and was "overcome by the Spirit of the Lord."

She fell back and hit her head on the floor. She sued the church claiming the church was negligent and that the pastor committed libel and slander against her. She was awarded $315,000.00, but later an appeals court reduced it to $40,000.00, awarding negligence only. She claims that as a result of the fall, she suffers emotional and physical problems.

As you can see from this lawsuit that even in the course of spiritual flow of a service, a lawsuit can result. We strongly suggest that, in every consideration and recommendation that we have made in this book, you consult with a professional for any specific training and expertise needed in a particular area.

It should also be noted some lawsuits will not be avoided because of the litigious society that we live in. However, with due diligence in all areas of ministry life, the great majority of them will never be successful.

Examples include such things as:

1. Site security assessment: There is no such thing as a cookie cutter plan to cover safety and security in every church in the same manner. Anyone telling you this either does not understand church security or does not have your overall best interest at heart. Having a qualified site security assessment completed will expose any vulnerability in your house of worship. This will allow you to plan and address specific areas of concern and not waste time, effort or money using a one size fits all approach.

2. Fire Safety Assessment: It is highly advised that you contact your local fire department and have them conduct a fire safety assessment. Some of the things they will deal with are the amount and placement of fire extinguishers, making sure all your exit signs and emergency lighting is in place and panic bars on egress doors where necessary. Many have avoided this needed assessment out of fear that the local fire department may limit the number of occupants that can assemble at a given size building or room. However, in the event of a fire if the church can be proven not to have met code, they can be held accountable in a court of law.

3. EMTs: As the people of the church get older medical emergencies can become more of an issue. American Red Cross: CPR, AED, and First Responder training are often overlooked when it comes to assuring safety of the members and visitors of your house of worship. It is recommended that you certify as many staff members as are willing in CPR, first responder and AED training if your church has one. It is a good practice to note who are the Doctors, Nurses and even EMT's in your church. Knowing who to call on in an emergency may buy you precious time before the EMT's show up in the event of a medical emergency.

4. **Local Police Department:** When unforeseen circumstances occur, you want the peace of mind that your local police department will respond expeditiously. Building a solid relationship with the police will ensure that response time is swift. In some cases it is advisable to share your emergency response plans to certain scenarios with your local police department. This will help them with their response. Having a relationship with the local police also keeps them aware of your church service times. That way they know if they are responding when the house of worship is occupied or empty.

The most important factor to consider in these recommendations is that by addressing your vulnerabilities you are mitigating the risk to yourself, your congregation and the church building itself.

As we have illustrated in this book, there has been a rise in emergent incidences in churches that would require the use of safety and security measures in the church. This is the concept that we are focusing on in this book.

We understand that the numbers show that they majority of the people who attend churches do so in churches with less than 100 people. With that being the case, there are usually limited financial resources available to pay for and employ full-time security staff to manage all of these different situations. We want to instill the proactive mindset within the body of the church so that it is viewed as such from the outside and will help ward off most potential problems.

The proactive mindset deals with potential issues before they occur. Good church safety and security is pro-active, curious and sometimes may seem a bit cumbersome. It does not wait until there is a problem and then rush to fix it. Good pro-active safety and security looks at prevention and avoidance as its main goals, although there is a fall back plan if all else fails.

Please notice that in every emergency situation noted here, although the Church must have a good response to each type of event, it is always the best procedure to call 911 as well so that the proper authorities provide help and peace to regardless of the situation.

Glossary

Proactive measures: Proactive measures are those standards or procedures that you implement, employ or put in place that address potential problems before they happen. For instance, having a procedure of having all church office doors locked during service hours helps eliminate anyone having access to them when they are unoccupied by office personnel.

Proactive mindset: The capacity to constantly think in a manner that is focused on the safety and security of oneself, others and the environment and see the potential problem[s] well before it has occurred. Proactive mindset has the ability to see a series of values, put them together and foresee a potential problem. Then introduce protective measures to mitigate the issue before it happens.

Baseline behavior: Baseline behavior is that behavior that is consistent with the specific environment. Arriving at church in the winter months with an overcoat is acceptable due to the weather conditions and season, however, during the month of June would be inconsistent with the baseline behavior of the season. Standing up with your arms stretched toward heaven talking in the spirit can be baseline behavior in some churches, but would not be the same in another church.

Hard Target: Person, place or thing that has implemented obvious security measures, making it a difficult target to be compromised.

Soft Target: Person, place or thing that has little to no security measures, making it an easy target to be compromised. Hard Targets force an attacker to move their focus to a softer target.

Protective Mindset: The capacity to constantly think in a manner that is focused on the safety and security of yourself, others and the environment. Always recognizing when there is a potential to be compromised and then make changes to fix it.

Church Safety: Measures implemented to protect the church staff, members and visitors from physical or mental harm through intentional harm, unintentional harm or negligence.

Fence: Particular person or place that provides an avenue to purchase stolen goods

De-escalation: A process of mitigating a potential crisis or incident by averting a troubled person's attention to you where you can use empathy by listening to, and talking the person through the situation at hand.

Aggressive Friendliness: To be overly friendly and attentive with the idea of letting the person know you clearly recognize who they are.

Red Behavior: Is a behavior that is unexpected or inconsistent with normal behavior or conduct in that specific environment. For example, someone walking into your church wearing a winter coat during the summer months would be considered red behavior. It doesn't necessarily mean the person intends to do harm, but there is an obvious inconsistency with the behavior and the environment.

Frequently Asked Questions

1. **As a member of a congregation, what is it that I should be looking for to spot potential danger while attending church service? For Pastor Andrew, how can I balance being present in the service without being overly watchful to the point that I am distracted?**

There is an innate six sense that we all possess. It is more sensitive in some more than others. If you are a regular member of a church you more than likely attend church the same time each week and probably sit in the same general area. The faces of the members in that general area become familiar to you. As time goes on you become accustomed to a baseline behavior of how they attend church. Some days they are very cordial and greet you with a smile. At other times they seem to be weighed down with something on their mind. Subconsciously you know that this shift in mood and behavior is consistent with church behavior. EMBRACE THAT GIFT. You often take notice of any behavior above or below what you have already established as your own baseline. What you have done without even knowing is policed your area in the church.

Once the order of the service begins you have a very good idea of how the service will flow up to the pastor delivering the message. In this order of service you, without even recognizing, have also mentally recorded behavior consistent with the flow of the service.

Once the order of the service begins you have a very good idea of how the service will unfold to the point that the pastor is delivering the message. In this order of service you, without even realizing it, have also mentally recorded the behavior consistent with the flow of the service.

There are other behaviors that most individuals notice that we want them to embrace in the overall safety and security of the church. For instance, if you observe a person wearing a long wool coat during the summer, you understand that is inconsistent with the season. If you see someone seated in the church wearing a cap and sunglasses, it does not mean that they intend to do harm, but the behavior is inconsistent with your usual environment and they should be approached by church staff. In the security industry we call this situational awareness.

Our intent is to encourage the entire church community to work together in this effort and bring to the attention of church staff those behaviors that seem inconsistent with the usual baseline behavior of the church. The more eyes we have working together in this effort, the safer and more secure your church experience becomes. More importantly, we are encouraging that in our approach all members act upon what they notice and make notification. E.K.

Certainly the main reason we go to church is not to focus on problems, but to focus on worshipping the Lord. As Eric says, "Once you feel your situation fits into what you feel is the normal baseline of your area of church, you must trust God that others also are doing the same thing, usually without even trying." Most importantly, if someone sees something it is vital that they say something. I might also add as you make your way through the building observe for anything unusual... if you see something say something. However, once you are seated in God's presence, it's time to trust Him to keep you safe as well as the other members of the church and staff who are also doing their part. A.P.S.

2. I notice a lot of entrances and exits in and out of church. How do you determine the amount of security that is adequate and appropriate for a church service?

The number of doors in a church should not determine the amount of safety and security staffed. For the most part churches are not concerned with access control where you have to have a ticket to attend. There is, however, a possibility that some churches may want the flow or members to enter and depart certain doors in order to manage the flow of attendees. In this case there should be some consideration on manning those doors that you do not want to be used as ingress or egress. In these incidences, volunteers can be used to assist in the overall intent. Empowering someone with this task goes a long way with the overall vigilance in your church members.

There is no exact formula to produce the absolute number of security staff to church member ratio. Some experts say that for every 100 members you should have an additional staff member assigned to church security. This formula may work perfectly for a shareholders meeting or some other special event, however, in dealing with churches we have to consider, resources and availability of trained personnel.

3. Should churches hire uniformed or off-duty police to serve as security?

There are no absolutes to this answer, however we need to be clear that having a police presence is not an absolute deterrence in someone doing harm or committing a crime. Secondly, the average uniformed police officer is not specifically trained to perform proactive security measures. To be fair, however, there are some specialized units within some departments that are specifically trained to perform personnel protection. All police departments do not have these units, thereby leaving the pool of available officers to perform security to that of the street cop.

When a church decides to use these officers it may serve as a comfort to the people, however the church may not understand what their true security abilities are.

In some ways, having a uniformed presence can actually assist if someone who wants to do harm. There is a pre-incident period where some level of surveillance is conducted to ascertain if the plan can be successfully completed. Having uniformed police can actually assist a person in knowing where the security presence is and therefore move the bad guy to a different location in the building to carry out his evil intent.

4. If I observe suspicious activity what should I do?

The first thing you want to do is contact the first church employee/servant you see and carefully articulate what you observed. It is very important that you relay accurate information regarding your observations so that there is no misunderstanding in the conversation.

It is key that you convey specifically what you saw or heard and not allow yourself to imply anything that you did not see or hear.

Taking note of what this person looks like as well as clothing colors and styles they wore can be very helpful to those given the task of finding this person as quickly as possible.

CONTACT THE AUTHORS

Dr. Andrew P. Surace – hopedealer007@aol.com
Eric Konohia – CMAS, CMEPS – ekonohia@bpigroupusa.com

NOTES

www.ingramcontent.com/pod-product-compliance
Lightning Source LLC
Chambersburg PA
CBHW072054290426
44110CB00014B/1674